WHO'S YOUR PILOT?

Choosing the *Right* Financial Advisor for You

Richard J. Feola, CRPC®

Sharpe Ratio Publishing
ISBN 13: 978-1-945028-09-0

Cover design by Shawna Feola
Production assistance by Adam Robinson
for Good Book Developers

An ebook version of this book is available for free at
www.retirementsecondopinion.net

The information contained in this book is for informational
purposes only and is not a solicitation to buy or sell any of
the products mentioned. The information is not intended to
be used as the sole basis for financial decisions, nor should it
be construed as advice designed to meet the particular needs
of an individual's situation.

You can contact the author's team for a complimentary second opinion service as outlined in chapter 2. You'll need your
latest investment statements as well as two years of your most
recent tax returns. Contact Richard Feola at *rich@fffgonline.
com* for more information, or to schedule a visit if you're in
the New Jersey area.

To all of my family: thank you for all of your love and support, especially my wife Shawna for understanding the time that was spent on this project.

To all individuals and families looking for unbiased retirement advice in today's day and age.

I'd also like to thank Kathleen A. Nolan—the very best mentor I could ask for in this business—for all of the hours she spent teaching me through her integrity, honesty, transparency, and extensive experience. It is a pleasure working with you every day.

To Kelly Meyerhoff: Thank you for brainstorming with me and coming up with creative ways to use the pilot analogy.

And to the rest of our team, thank you for all of your support!

Contents

Preface

G ROWING UP, I ALWAYS LOOKED up to my grandfather. He was a successful entrepreneur and do-it-yourself investor, and he always used to talk to me about his investments. It never interested me, as I was much more interested in playing sports or playing my guitar, so whenever grandpa would go on and on about his stock picks, I just nodded along.

But I remember one day quite vividly. I was sitting on the couch with my grandfather watching the stock ticker tape roll off each quote. "Cisco is going to change technology forever," he said in an excited and fervent voice. "They're developing fiber optic cables which will transmit information faster than we've ever known." It was 1998, and my grandfather was passionate about his hot stock picks. And hot they were! Cisco was at $16 per share, and within a few short months it shot up to over $79 (and went through a number of stock splits over the next couple of years). The thrill my grandfather experienced is known by most who attempt to make a fortune with their investments. Once you get a few wins under your belt, you feel invincible. The confidence and emotional attachment he felt to these tech companies was hard to let go of, and in only a few short years he watched Cisco go all the way back down to $10 a share (he had sold out many months earlier, but not without locking in significant losses). Going through a bear market sure does humble you, I'd say!

There was one thing I never forgot about grandpa. The stress and anguish he carried was unparalleled. In spite of his experience as a successful entrepreneur and investor, and the small fortune he made as a businessman, I saw the fear in his eyes when things started crashing in the early 2000s. He watched the TV even more closely than ever before, yearning and hoping things would turn around. And they did after a few years.

Then when I was a senior in high school, my grandpa gave me a book on investing which changed my life. All I wanted to do was buy stocks with my extra money, and I wanted to one day become a millionaire like him. I was inspired to follow in his footsteps as an entrepreneur and amateur investor.

Right after I graduated college, the housing bubble started to collapse. And when global markets followed suit in the financial crisis, I distinctly remember my grandfather starting to get stressed like never before. He never knew when the bottom would hit because the market just kept dropping. Long story short, he made some bad decisions since he was fully retired and had to rely on distributions from his accounts. He couldn't afford to wait it out because he needed the income and was forced to take distributions. Unfortunately, he only lived for a few more years. The stress and anguish he faced over his investments, I believe, caused him to lose heart and this affected his health. He tried over those few short years to make his money back, but it was too late. He couldn't recover from that big of a loss.

At his funeral, it hit me. I found my purpose. My grandpa's unfortunate turn of fate is what inspired me to become a financial advisor for retirees. I now wanted to ensure that other people would not face the anxiety that my grandpa experienced. The financial crisis was now over and the economy was starting to improve, but I knew that the economy was cyclical, and that eventually this process might happen again. I needed to make sure that my clients were properly positioned to face that.

But since joining this industry, I've learned a few things. I've learned how this business works and I am absolutely convinced of one thing, and it is the most important decision you may ever make before or after you retire: who you choose as your financial advisor is one of the most important financial decisions of your life. It really is! You need to make sure you get this right. Don't you want the best of the best? This is your life savings we're talking about.

And honestly, I may never have written this book if I weren't blessed to have had the life I've been given. I'm a firm believer in "everything happens for a reason," and the opportunities and experiences I've been able to glean from my mentors in this business have been paramount to my success. I've seen the good, the bad, and the ugly. I've worked for the insurance companies (when I first started out), the brokerage houses, and have transitioned to becoming independent. I've seen it all. Now I'm here to help you decide how to determine if the financial advisor you're interviewing is the right fit for *you*.

Do you like to travel? When you do, do you take an airplane? A pilot is someone we can all relate to. What do you expect when you step foot on that plane? Well, you're probably expecting a few things:

1. That the pilot is an upstanding citizen;
2. That the pilot is qualified;
3. That the pilot has no ulterior motives;
4. That the pilot has availed himself of all the resources that will help make your flight as smooth as possible;
5. That the pilot can adequately use his instruments for navigation;
6. That the pilot has a team in place to help him in the areas he cannot always attend to;
7. That the pilot can minimize turbulence if the flight gets rocky;
8. That the pilot can handle a worst-case scenario;
9. That the pilot communicates if something goes wrong;
10. And last, that you actually enjoy the flight experience!

These are just some examples of what you might expect from your pilot. I think this is a great analogy for choosing a financial advisor because it's so relatable. I hope you find this book helpful in your search for your financial advisor in life. You need to get this right! There are too many who find this out the hard way, and it often costs them a whole lot of money in the process. As the old proverb says, "wise men learn from the mistakes of others, but fools learn from their own."

—To your success in finding your pilot,
Richard J. Feola, CRPC®

1. Your Biggest Concern: You Want Someone Trustworthy

W HEN YOU STEP ONTO THE plane, you have the utmost faith and confidence in your pilot even though you've never met them in your life. Have you ever thought about that? You would never think that the pilot had any ulterior motives about getting you to your destination. After all, it's their job, right? They get paid to fly you to where you want to go. But clearly some pilots must be better than others, don't you think? Some who had better grades, or more experience, or are more proficient in reading their instruments than others.

Imagine you want to take a flight from New York City to Los Angeles. Your desire is to get there as soon as possible. But let's imagine we're in a different world. In this world, the airports pay the pilots, not the airlines. Each airport gives incentives to their pilots. And if they have a contract with another airport, like Milwaukee, then the Milwaukee airport will give the pilot a little more pay if they stop in their airport before going to Los Angeles. In this world, it doesn't matter how fast *you* get to your destination, because the pilots are incentivized to stop at other airports for connecting flights. So even though you could have taken a non-stop flight from NYC to LA, you may stop in one, two, or even three different airports before you get there! Why? Because the pilots are compensated based on how many stops they make. Do you see how this changes the story? It's no longer about you; it's about *them*.

And herein lies the source of the financial industry's bad reputation. Wall Street doesn't necessarily care about you. Oh, I'm sorry. Did you think they did? No! They make money whether the market is up or down. They don't only make money when you make money. They make a lot of their money on the buying and the selling. To return to the analogy, many of them get paid on the connecting flights. This is why brokers or registered representatives are sometimes looked at like "snake oil salesmen." It's deeply embedded in the history of Wall Street. A lot of folks feel that investment bankers and brokers always seem richer than everyone else, and this *bothers* us. "Why are they making money and I can't seem to get by?" Have you ever felt that way? You're not alone.

So, the first and most important attribute in your financial advisor should always be trustworthiness. And this can be hard to gauge, because everybody seems like a nice guy, right? Well, this is where you have to go with what you should always trust: your gut! Not only that, but do the research necessary to find a trustworthy financial advisor. I hope to show you in this book the most fundamental attributes you should look for in your search.

There have been many different consumer reports done by various custodians and investment related organizations. In nearly all of them, the clients who were interviewed thought that trustworthiness was the most important characteristic in their financial advisor.

So, what are some ways to determine if your financial advisor can be trusted?

1) They Tell You The Truth

It can be really difficult to find a financial advisor who is going to "tell it like it is," and be straightforward and honest with you. How do you know if someone is telling the truth or not? In this book, I'm going to help you see past all the nonsense and get to the heart of the matter. How do you know if you've found the real deal? You want a financial advisor who will be real with you. One who will tell you the truth, even if it hurts! One who will not just try to pull the wool over your eyes and make a quick sale.

Part of this can be seen when they go through their first few consultations with you. Nearly all of my clients are between the ages of 55 and 75, and are either already retired, or retirement is soon approaching. Most baby boomers are concerned about whether or not they've saved enough to retire comfortably. Did your financial advisor ever give you a straight answer on that? It's a yes or no question. Either you've saved enough, or you haven't. It's kind of like asking the pilot, "Do we have enough gas to get to our destination?" It's a yes or no! The pilot will not take off without knowing that he will have enough gas to get you where you're going. And if there isn't enough gas, he will do whatever is necessary to make sure that it gets taken care of.

Now, can a financial advisor make money come from thin air? Of course not. But if someone is straightforward with you, they will tell you if you have a problem, and then design a plan to help you fix it (and they should also tell you if they can't fix it). If you look at your dealings with a previous advisor and they either didn't put a plan together for you or didn't tell you if you're on course to hit your goal, then I think it's time you find a new pilot. You don't want to run out of gas 30,000 feet above sea level, do you?

Another important factor of telling you the truth is that they are up front about their compensation from the beginning. If a potential advisor is not straightforward with you about how they are compensated, then for me that is a huge red flag that they may not be serving your best interests.

2) They Find Out What Is Most Important to You, and Why

Think back to when you first sat down with a financial advisor. How did the conversation begin? Did they start out by talking about their company, or about themselves? Or even worse, did you go right into a conversation about a product or investment? Clearly, you can see what the priority is here. Now, most won't stoop that low (at least I hope not). Maybe they asked you a series of questions about your financial situation. They can't advise you if they don't know what's going on, right? Well, that seems noble. A doctor wouldn't give you a prescription without taking your vitals; this is true. But I think the right advisor has to go one step further. They have to learn not merely about your financial circumstances, but about your life! They should find out about your marriage and your family. They should find out how many grandkids you have, where they live, and what you like to do with them. They should ask about what you like to do on the weekends, or where your passion is found.

Your conversation may get sidetracked for twenty minutes just talking about how much you love your family, or how much you like to hike, or how much you enjoy music. In my opinion, the best advisors should ask questions like, "How did you earn your first dollar?" "What was money like when you were growing up?" "What does money mean to you?" They should find out about what's most important to you and what you value the most about your wealth. It is only when your advisor finds out what's most important to you that they will be able to get a vision of how to help you pursue it. Like my greatest mentor in this business once told me, "It's not until they know how much you care that they will care about how much you know." When I first sit down with a prospective client, I don't talk about a single financial thing until at least 30-45 minutes in! You're more than just a dollar sign! You are a beautiful person created in the image of God, and a good financial advisor (pilot) should find out why you want to go to your destination before they show you how they'll help guide you on your journey.

3) They Don't Have a History Of Bad Behavior

As the old saying goes, "You can't teach an old dog new tricks." If a pilot had a history of bad takeoffs or landings, wouldn't you want to know about it? Or what if the pilot went off course a few times from their coordinates and almost caused a catastrophe? In the same way, some financial advisors have been known to cut corners. Maybe they left out an important detail to a client, or they misappropriated the client's funds, or maybe they just flat out lied. The regulators of the financial industry are always busy—there's always someone to catch doing something wrong. It's sad, but true! Now, I'm not suggesting that every advisor is bad, or even that most of them are. But as with any industry that works on commission and fees, there will always be the few bad apples. And you need to know how to spot them.

When I worked as a broker, one of my managers seemed like a really nice guy (and for all illustrative purposes in this book I will call him "Johnny B. Bad"—after the old Chuck Berry song). He was funny, he was confident, and he seemed to know what he was talking about. But when I looked him up online, I saw that he had more than a few clients complain about various things, and he had fines against him. From that day on, I lost respect for him. And it wasn't long after that that I stopped being a broker altogether. A lot can be learned about someone if you find out that they have a history of misrepresentation or regulatory disciplinary actions.

The regulators have actually created websites in order for you to check up on your financial advisor. One of them is FINRA's BrokerCheck; this is specifically for registered representatives who sell investment products. Former brokers are listed there as well. But you may not see the advisor you're interviewing on BrokerCheck (if they're not a broker—or if you do, it may only show their years of experience as a broker specifically, even though they may have many more years under their belt in the industry). If they're a true financial advisor, they will be a fiduciary advisor or investment adviser representative and they will be listed at SEC.gov. Some are listed on both (if they're both an investment adviser representative (fiduciary) and a broker—an oxymoron to say the least—we will go more in depth on this matter and how to tell the difference between the two in chapter three. I will show you ways to tell the difference by just looking at their business card!).

Now, don't get me wrong. There are probably hundreds of thousands of financial advisors who really are trustworthy and honest. They're good people, and they want to help their clients and not hurt them. But being trustworthy and honest is not all that's required. That should be the foundation, no doubt, but there is so much more needed in the person you choose to help you manage your life savings. Unfortunately, some of these advisors may not even be aware of their potential shortfalls. And it's not always their fault! Many of them may not even know there is a different way. And even some who do know of a better way still choose to not go that route (which I will cover in chapter 4).

We've only covered the first aspect of your pilot: you need to trust them. Before you step on that plane you need to not even think twice about their ability to put your best interests first.

RECAP: YOUR FINANCIAL ADVISOR SHOULD ...

1.   Be trustworthy, honest, and an upstanding citizen.

2. You Want Someone Knowledgeable

E VERYONE HOPES THEIR PILOT HAS more than a few takeoffs or landings under their belt. Everyone desires that their pilot is qualified enough to handle anything that may come along. It's the same with your financial advisor. Qualifications are very important! But, like we mentioned in the last chapter, their behavior is more important than how many letters are after their name.

The second biggest concern investors have is that they want their advisor to be knowledgeable. You can work with the most sincere, honest, and trustworthy advisor in the world, but if they lack experience or knowledge, it's not worth much. It's no surprise that clients want their advisors to know what they're talking about; this is especially true for those clients who have less knowledge of the financial services realm.

Some brokers, agents and advisors may seem like they know what they're talking about, but be careful. The fact is that many people can pass a test if they study hard enough. Over the years, the regulators have made the licensing exams in our industry significantly more difficult (in order to help ensure those who advise clients on how to manage their money are better qualified), but the reality is still that many can pass a test. Just because someone has the proper qualifications on paper does not prove that they will be the right financial advisor for you; it only shows that they studied hard and may be a good test-taker. Does further education hurt? No, not at all! Don't get me wrong. But there are plenty of times when I see a prospective client's portfolio and I scratch my head and say, "This broker has two or three more certifications than me, and he did this with their money? What in the world was he thinking?" We all came into this industry the same way: we studied hard and figured out how we'd pass difficult tests. But passing a test and having experiential knowledge are two different things, and you need to be able to tell the difference.

I remember the day I passed my Series 7 securities exam and officially became a broker. I had previous experience with life insurance companies offering their standard products, but I had never dealt with the stock market or any investments up to that point. I remember when I told my manager, Johnny B. Bad, that I had passed my Series 7 exam on the first try.

"Great Job, Rich!" he said. "Now you can burn the book. Forget everything you learned."

I quickly responded, "Excuse me? Isn't this stuff I learned important?"

He reassured me, "It doesn't matter anymore. You're through the gate. You will learn the ropes from us. You won't need your study materials anymore."

So, as you might imagine, right off the bat I was a little nervous, as any rookie would be. (By the way, I didn't take his advice!) But herein lies the problem: many brokers and agents learn a significant portion of information and then get trained by their parent company to serve their company's agenda. I see this as a systemic problem. Now, it's certainly not in every case that this happens, but much of the knowledge and experience that many learn may not be what's reflected in their work. The client's best interests oftentimes are left at the wayside.

So, what are some ways that you can determine if your financial advisor is truly knowledgeable? How can you tell the difference between the salesmen and the strategist?

1) They Emphasize Strategy, Not Product

This is so essential! Ever go to a chicken dinner workshop? You know, where the presenter buys you dinner and tells you about their company or their solutions? If they mention anything about a product, or a specific financial tool, you might want to run for the hills! In my opinion, these individuals are focused on one thing only: selling you a product. A true financial advisor should demonstrate that they are agnostic about product and that strategy is what matters. He or she should strive to help you work towards your goals, no matter which products or investments comprise their recommendations. Ultimately, every client is in a different situation. There is no product in the world which will solve all your problems! Those advisors who have no bias one way or the other are, in my opinion, the only advisors with knowledge worth respecting. Did you hear the first lesson? They shouldn't offer a product without first explaining their strategy. And they can't strategize without first digging deep with you and finding out what your goals are.

2) They Offer a Thorough Second Opinion

Every financial advisor, in my opinion, should respect the loyalty you have with whoever is currently handling your money. After all, I would hope and pray that my clients would be loyal to me as well. But when you're interviewing a new advisor, what are they offering you? If they're the real deal, they will give you a thorough second opinion service. They will share the pros, cons, and the finest details of your current financial plan (or lack thereof). What are some things that might be included in a service like that?

An Income & Expense Analysis

If you're planning to retire someday, you want someone who will analyze your current cash flow and project how long your money should last in retirement. This can be done in a variety of ways, whether by income and expense software or by "Monte Carlo analysis." If your current advisor hasn't done one or the other yet, you have to ask "why not?" Isn't doing whatever is possible to help ensure that your money will last important? You don't want to run out of money before you run out of living! The pilot needs to determine whether or not there's enough fuel in the engine to make it to the end.

A Thorough Investment Snapshot

You also need someone who will show you the percentages of which asset classes represent your portfolio, and how they are correlated. This will show you how diversified you are, or if you're not fully diversified. Oftentimes in my experience when I do this analysis for my prospective clients, they are very surprised that they are not as diversified as they think.

This should also track the best and worst case scenarios, so you know what you might expect in the future. Many of these reports can track your investments' yield, returns, and many other important details that can affect you going forward. This way you can know if you're on track to hit your goals.

A Detailed Risk Analysis: How Much Are You Willing to Lose
Most advisors ask their clients if they're conservative, moderate, or aggressive. But those categories mean different things to different people! You may say you're moderate because you want a little higher return, but if the market starts plummeting, you lose sleep at night because you're taking on too much risk. The knowledgeable advisor should ask you a simple question, but to answer it is sometimes the hardest thing in the world. The question is this: "How much are you willing to lose in your investments in a single year?" It needs to be quantified as a dollar value. Once you figure out what that number is, then that makes it real. Saying you're aggressive doesn't make the losses real. You need to own how much risk you're willing to accept and a good advisor will be careful to find out that answer before they make any recommendations. A risk analysis can show you if your actual tolerance for risk matches up with how your current advisor has you positioned. If the numbers don't match, then you have to ask yourself: "Why didn't my advisor make sure I was comfortable with this level of risk?" It may not be until your accounts start going south that you finally notice these things, because they've become reality at that point. It's best to find out before that happens! Re-read that again. I'm serious. You may save some money!

A Complete Fee Analysis

If your pilot put watered down fuel into the engine, what would happen? Wouldn't the gas burn too quickly? The same is the reality with fees. They can eat away at your nest egg if not fairly balanced. Certain mutual fund investments in particular are known for not only the management fees and sales loads, but also they can have other costs associated with them (such as transaction costs, commissions, and market impact costs). It's important for you to understand all of the costs associated with your investments. In addition to the inherent costs of the investments, you want to make sure any advisory fees are also fairly balanced. Sometimes consumers are unaware of all the costs associated because mutual fund fees are separate and in addition to advisory fees. This is the case with certain other investment products as well—there can be inherent costs but also an advisory wrap fee on top of it all! If you have a large portion of cash in your portfolio, make sure your advisor isn't charging you on that portion. Money market accounts are barely paying any interest today, so you'd probably be better off holding the money in your own money market account for free than to pay a fee to your advisor for holding it (but many fiduciary advisors will hold large portions of cash for free as well).

A knowledgeable advisor should discuss all these things objectively with you and with a great deal of commentary surrounding how current economic events may impact your portfolio going forward. They should go over your main concerns, but they should also bring up concerns that you may be unaware of. That's what a second opinion is all about.

3) They Specialize in a Specific Area

You want to make sure you're working with a holistic advisor, one who understands the whole array of financial planning. But, in my opinion, the best of the best tend to have a specific niche that they specialize in. I knew an advisor who got divorced and was familiar with divorce court, and knew how to assist female divorcees on how to manage their finances after such a difficult process. There are financial advisors who specialize in 401k plans for business owners, so that's pretty much all they do. Then there are other people who focus solely on college education funding. If you're approaching retirement, or are already retired, then you may want to find an advisor whose niche is retirement income distribution strategies. The bottom line is this: you want to find the right advisor for what you are trying to accomplish. One problem with working with a generalist is that they are a jack of all trades, but (potentially) a master of none. You need someone who has an advanced knowledge of your situation, and has helped many others before you in similar circumstances.

SOME QUESTIONS TO ASK A POTENTIAL ADVISOR:

1. What niche market do you specialize in?
2. What is the age range of most of your clients?
3. What is an average household net worth under your management?
4. How many clients do you have?
5. Why did you choose to focus on this category of individuals and families?

6.   Do you focus on accumulation or preservation?

7.   What is your investment philosophy?

I'd like to mention one thing about experience. There is no doubt in my mind that doing actual financial planning trumps four years in college or passing a few tests or certifications. But, being a younger guy myself (I am currently in my 30s—at the time this book was published), I'd like to say that I believe it's more about who an advisor's mentor is rather than how much experience they may have. For instance, when I went independent and joined the firm I'm with now, I was unaware of many of the things I'm describing in this book. I was a generalist, I was a broker, I was trained poorly, and I experienced that whole side of the industry. But when I became independent, and got a new mentor (who, in my opinion, is one of the best financial advisors in the country, with extensive experience over 41 years), I really started learning what it means to be a great financial advisor. The network of advisors that we associate with are what I consider the most advanced and knowledgeable advisors that I have ever heard of. I mean I'm talking about extremely successful and knowledgeable business owners and advisors, and rubbing elbows with them helped me surge with experience.

I remember going over a particular strategy with my mentor one day and she said, "Rich, you know that you may have never learned this strategy for at least another 20 years if you stayed at your brokerage house—or maybe never at all." It's the truth! I learned more in a couple months after becoming independent then I had known in all my previous experience up to that point! That's why I consider myself so lucky and blessed, and why I'm so passionate about showing people how to find the right advisor. Imagine if a young rookie pilot was able to be alongside Air Force fighter-jet pilots and fly planes with them every day. All he knew before were the small planes that were easier to fly, but now that he's hanging with the big boys—what do you think will happen? Don't you think this young pilot will start flying better than before? You tend to become like those you spend time with. It's no different than with your financial advisor and the network that they have surrounded themselves with.

But there is one important thing to remember when it comes to experience and knowledge, and I know this first-hand. I have seen some advisors, many of them in their late 60s and 70s, who are just so stuck in the past it's unbelievable. They haven't kept up with the ever-changing industry, they haven't embraced the benefits of technology, and they are still managing money like they did 20, 30 or even 40 years ago. As a result, I feel their old-fashioned ways have made them irrelevant. This may even apply to some in their 40s and 50s too! So don't necessarily be put off if an advisor might be on the younger side, or even significantly younger than you. They may have a better grasp on the current economic climate or have the ability to leverage technology even better than some of the more experienced advisors in the industry.

I always say, "there's two people you want to be younger than you in life: your doctor and your financial advisor!" Isn't that the truth? You don't want your doctor to croak before you do, and I believe the same rings true for your financial advisor. They need to be there for when you go up to heaven so that your spouse and your kids are taken care of too. This also applies to advisors who are approaching retirement. Have they put a transition plan in place? What happens if they plan to retire, who will take their place? Do you like who's on their team? My mentor has thought this through and has created a transition plan for her practice, but you'd be surprised at how many advisors do not prepare their clients for their own retirement from the financial planning business.

Don't be too concerned. You'll be able to tell if someone knows what they're talking about. A knowledgeable and experienced financial advisor should tell you if you're in good shape or if he or she thinks you need help. Maybe it's not that you're positioned improperly, but perhaps there are just some services that you are in need of which your current advisor does not offer (like tax strategies, advanced income distribution strategies, or estate planning concepts). Follow your gut instinct. Never be afraid to ask a potential advisor questions. They should have adequate and satisfactory answers for all of your concerns. If they don't, then move on!

RECAP: YOUR FINANCIAL ADVISOR SHOULD ...

1. Be trustworthy, honest, and an upstanding citizen.

2. Be knowledgeable about your current situation, and be able to show you how they can better assist you. Professional certifications are helpful, but not necessary.

3. You Want a Fiduciary

R EMEMBER OUR EXAMPLE OF THE connecting flights at the start of this book? It's so important that your financial pilot have no ulterior motives or incentives to offer one solution over another. This is what it means to be a fiduciary and to do what's always in the client's best interest.

The word fiduciary comes from the Latin word fiducia which means "trust." A fiduciary advisor should be a trusted advisor. It's someone who you know is legally obligated to put your best interests at the forefront of every recommendation. The word "fiduciary" has become a real buzzword these past few years ever since the Department of Labor introduced its new "fiduciary rule" which requires all financial advisors, brokers and insurance agents who work with qualified retirement plans to always do what is in the client's best interest. I wholeheartedly agree with the idea that all financial professionals should be fiduciaries in order to help protect consumers from receiving bad advice. It's strange to think that it's even possible to not do what's in the client's best interest and get away with it, but this is the world we live in.

So, if a financial professional is not a fiduciary, then what is he or she? There are two standards in the financial industry: 1) the fiduciary standard and 2) the suitability standard.

The fiduciary standard holds all investment adviser representatives (those with series 65 or 66 securities registrations and who are affiliated with a Registered Investment Advisory firm) to the highest standard of accountability in putting their clients' needs first. Any recommendations which are made must be what is best for the client, even if it proves less beneficial for the financial advisor.

The suitability standard means that the broker or insurance agent is required to offer recommendations which are "suitable," even though it may not be in the client's best interest. For instance, some suitability parameters are those such as age, risk tolerance, liquidity requirements, investment objectives, and an acknowledgement from the client that they will accept whichever costs are associated with the investment or insurance product.

So technically, a broker or insurance agent could offer you a financial product not because it is the best option for you, but because you are age 60, you said you're a moderate investor, and you desire your money to grow—and it is considered suitable for your situation based on the advisor's analysis of your needs. A suitability standard doesn't necessarily mean you are getting something that is bad for you, of course, but it does leave the door open for conflicts of interest, in which your broker or insurance agent could make a recommendation that nets him or her the largest commission. Any time you have a conflict of interest like this, there is the potential that you won't receive the financial products that are best for you from among those available to the broker or insurance agent.

And this is why there has been such a big controversy

around this topic. For example, many broker-dealers have close ties with certain mutual fund companies, and have agreements known as "revenue sharing." For instance, broker-dealer ABC may incentivize their brokers to offer company XYZ's mutual funds (because XYZ says they will direct all their trading to broker-dealer ABC). If the financial advisor who works for ABC offers company XYZ's mutual fund, then they will get a higher commission than if they offer a mutual fund from company DEF. But what if the DEF mutual fund is better for you? Do you think the broker will offer it? Maybe, but maybe not—there's a meaningful incentive not to.

In addition, there are different classes of mutual funds (A, B, and C). They compensate the broker in different ways. Sometimes when I analyze a prospective client's portfolio, I see that they have a lot of C funds. C funds tend to have the highest long-term, ongoing cost of any mutual fund. If they were intended to be held longer than two or three years, then I believe that the broker should have considered an A fund. An A fund has a larger up front cost; but over the long-term it often ends up costing the investor less over time. I've seen clients hold C funds for many years. Why? There could be a number of reasons, but in some cases I have seen that the broker wanted a higher revenue stream over a longer period of time rather than being paid once up front. This happens! There are rules and regulations in place to try and reduce the risk of this, but it can be difficult to monitor.

This is often the case with many proprietary funds or products as well. Although it's not required for a broker to offer only proprietary funds or products, the incentives they receive can affect their decision making process. For instance, a broker may receive better 401k or healthcare benefits for meeting sales quotas which exist for these proprietary products. Also, the training and education these brokers receive is sometimes skewed to promote these proprietary products and funds which benefit the parent company's bottom line. Unfortunately, if your advisor is subject to the suitability standard alone, they are not subject to a higher standard of transparency and full disclosure.

So, how can you tell if someone is held to the fiduciary or the suitability standard? Wouldn't you want to know before you choose your pilot? I will tell you how you may be able to tell, just by looking at their business card. But keep in mind, not all business cards are approved by a regulatory department or compliance division, so this may not be the only way to tell which standard your financial professional is subject to.

The Suitability Standard

If the financial professional's business card or website says something like this, then they are a broker under the suitability standard: "Securities offered by/through XYZ company, LLC, member FINRA/SIPC."

FINRA is the regulatory body that regulates brokers that adhere to the suitability standard. So, if you want to remember in short, just remember that word: FINRA.

If your financial professional only has an insurance license, then they will likely have a title like "Licensed Agent" or "Insurance Professional/Agent/Producer" on their business card. These professionals are limited to only offering insurance products and are held to the suitability standard as well. Insurance professionals are prohibited from referring to themselves as "advisors" or "financial advisors."

The Fiduciary Standard

Any financial professional who has this on their business card or website is a fiduciary: "Investment advisory services offered through XYZ Company, an SEC Registered Investment Adviser." The Securities and Exchange Commission (SEC) is the regulatory body that regulates investment adviser representatives that adhere to the fiduciary standard. If you only remember one thing, remember that abbreviation: SEC.

Now, it can be questionable if an advisor has *both* disclosures on their card. If that is the case, then they are subject to both the suitability and fiduciary standards. It may be difficult to know which recommendation is in your best interest, because not all of them have to be.

A fiduciary is required to be up front and tell you how they're compensated, usually in the first meeting. Many fiduciaries also charge planning fees for their services. You may have had experience with previous financial advisors who never charged you for their time. If they're not charging you for their time, then they're probably being compensated by earning commissions for selling you a financial product. If you go see an attorney or a CPA, they charge you by the hour, right? If a financial advisor doesn't tell you about their compensation it's a red flag because you know they are getting compensated in some way that may not benefit you.

Every pilot in the world has no conflict of interest; they just do their job. You want a financial advisor in life who will do theirs too. Unfortunately, the reputation of Wall Street is much different. Once again, your broker may be a wonderful person. They may be charitable, kindhearted, and down to earth. They may give great advice in whichever ways they are able to. But the reality is that there are pilots in this industry who are better equipped than others. Think of it this way: a pilot who works for one airline may be better equipped than one who works for another. One airline may have better planes, or give their pilots better tools in which to make each flight smoother. The big banks and brokerage houses have their agendas and sometimes their bottom line is more important than their clientele. They may never say that up front, but it's more about how they behave and how they train their brokers which tells the real truth about this dilemma.

SOME QUESTIONS TO ASK A POTENTIAL ADVISOR:

1. Are you a fiduciary?

2. How are you compensated?

3. Is there another investment or product which makes more sense for me?

4. How did you come to this recommendation?

5. Do you have any special incentives or sales quotas?

One sidenote on the Department of Labor fiduciary rule—this rule will most affect those brokers and insurance agents who operate under the suitability standard because they will now be forced to operate under the fiduciary standard. Unfortunately, the reach of this rule is only for retirement accounts. This means that brokers can still be under the suitability standard for investments outside of retirement accounts. Those who were fiduciaries before this bill will not be forced to change much, other than requiring some additional paperwork. Strong pullback from those sections of the financial services industry subject to the suitability standard has been due to the thought of having to change their entire standard of doing business—which of course will cost them money. Whether or not the rule remains in its current form, I believe it's still fundamental to work with a true fiduciary moving forward.

RECAP: YOUR FINANCIAL ADVISOR SHOULD ...

1. Be trustworthy, honest, and an upstanding citizen.

2. Be knowledgeable about your current situation, and be able to show you how they can better assist you. Professional certifications are helpful, but not necessary.

3. Uphold a fiduciary standard—which means they are fully transparent about their compensation and disclose any conflicts of interest. They are legally required to make recommendations which are in your best interest.

4. You Want Someone Independent

W HICH FLIGHT WOULD YOU CHOOSE: one where you have to sit in coach next to someone you'd rather not be next to (and be in the same situation on your connecting flight), or a private, customized jet with all the legroom you could want, traveling non-stop to your destination? It's obvious we'd rather have a custom flight. Similarly, working with a fiduciary advisor who is independent means that you are able to receive a financial plan that is tailor-fit and customized for your unique financial future.

Imagine that you went shopping at a wholesale club. But right down the street there is a competing wholesale club who offers the same products: groceries, home goods, etc. Every wholesale club also has their own proprietary products. These are products which are unique to that club. The wholesale club will not offer the paper towels or toilet paper that is unique to their competitor; they will offer their own. In other words, each wholesale club has a bias towards one product over another because these proprietary items are what makes them money. It would be bad business for one club to offer their competitor's products. Now, enter in whichever brokerage house, bank, or insurance company you want in this space: _____. They will tell their representatives to offer their own products or investments, even if they are inferior to others on the market. Why? Because it's what makes them money. They care about their bottom line. Now, don't get me wrong; many of their products may be suitable for you. Many of them may be similar to what you need. But that doesn't mean it's necessarily in your "best interest"—it just means it's what they've got to give.

The independent fiduciary, on the other hand, is of a different sort altogether. The independent has what is known as an "open architecture"—they are open to use whichever solution, investment, or product they believe makes the most sense for you. They don't work for any company in particular—they work for you. Do you see the difference? They are able to avail themselves of whatever resources are available in the open marketplace in order to help you. I like that kind of freedom, and it's what you need to consider when choosing your financial pilot.

I'd like to tell you a little story. At my previous firm, there was a broker who was known as the highest performing broker in the branch. Everyone respected him. He was a younger guy (also in his 30s), but he wore fancy custom suits and always reeked of cologne which probably cost $50 per spray. He was always the first one in the office and the last to leave. There was no doubt that he had an incredible work ethic. I'll call him Jeremiah Bullfrog.

One day, I had a meeting scheduled with a prospective client. It was planned that I would attend the meeting with my direct manager, Johnny B. Bad. But Johnny had something come up in his schedule, so he asked Jeremiah to join me. "Wow!" I thought. "I'm going to be able to see Jeremiah work his magic. Now I'll be able to find out how he does his job so well." So we met at the client's home and it was time to see the champ in action. He made some small talk for a while, but when it got down to business he started doing what he does best: pushing products. He didn't mention strategy, investment philosophy, nor did he even find out what the client's goals or concerns were. Right away, he began slinging product. But boy was he good. He talked about Real Estate Investment Trusts, and super-hot mutual funds, and variable annuities galore. He made everything sound so good, and it was hard to disagree with him. People just fell in his lap because he was such a good communicator, and he was able to explain how these products had such a good reputation (which is another debate in and of itself). He emphasized all the good things that these investments would do for the client, and when the time came, the client was ready to sign on the dotted line. I could feel the pressure in the room when he strongly emphasized the need for these products in the client's situation. And all the while I was wondering, "Is this what they really need, though?" I had an aching in my heart that told me something was drastically wrong about this scenario. He already knew what he was going to sell before he entered the room.

You see, our company had products and solutions which were specific to our group. And whether they were good or not is irrelevant. The fact is that even if there were better things out there that were available to him, Jeremiah would not mention those solutions because he wasn't trained to.

There are many class action lawsuits against some of the major financial companies for these types of situations (see www.classaction.org). In some cases, proprietary funds or products have been offered with misleading information or unrealistic illustrations, and these companies are starting to have to pay the piper. It goes without saying that this is a major problem, and there's no wonder the government is feeling they have to intervene in order to make it easier for consumers to get unbiased advice and have access to the financial solutions they so desperately need. The big firms of Wall Street have, in my opinion, been shown to not have the public's best interests at the forefront; hopefully that begins to change in the coming years. Once again, this is more than just a people problem. Your broker or agent may be a great person, and you trust them with your money, but if they work for what I view as a "broken" system, you may be getting the short end of the stick without even realizing it.

And sometimes, brokers are even aware of their company's shortfalls, but they still choose to go on doing business under that company because it is too stressful and difficult to change. Some brokers have been at the same company for 10, 20, or even 30 years, and have grown a large book of business. For them to jump ship and go independent might cost them a significant chunk of their ongoing revenue stream. Some of these brokers feel stuck—they know they should be independent for their clients' sake, but they are too afraid to make a change because they fear how it will affect their take-home pay.

Take some time and search Google for the phrase "revenue sharing disclosure." You will see major financial companies revealing their disclosures about revenue sharing. What is revenue sharing, you might ask? Revenue sharing is when a large firm has a compensation agreement with another financial company. For instance, the parent firm may incentivize their brokers to offer mutual funds from a certain mutual fund company. As part of the agreement, the firm will pay their brokers more for offering these funds, and the firm will receive additional compensation from the mutual fund company as well.

Not only that, but in these disclosures some companies explain these arrangements in a footnote or in the fine print of the disclosure describing the financial arrangement. For an example, search Google for the phrase "revenue sharing disclosure" again. One of the top search results will yield a large firm's revenue sharing disclosure. Due to copyright laws I cannot include the fine print in this book, but in one of the top search results you will see it listed. (With this company in particular, I'm sure you see their commercials all the time—they're the Jehovah Witnesses of the financial industry. No, really. They actually go door-to-door.)

To break it down for you simply, in the fine print it states that the mutual fund company in this agreement has not categorized all of the fees associated with these investments. However, for the fees which they can quantify, they will disclose how much of those fees are going back to the parent company and to their brokers. So, what do you think XYZ brokers are going to push? In many cases, they are going to push the funds which make them the most money. Are they the best out there? Maybe, maybe not. They're just the funds that have special incentives tied to them.

So, dear reader. This is what you're up against. This is why I feel it's so essential to work with someone who doesn't have these special incentives, or ulterior motives—someone independent, who works not for a specific company but directly for their clients.

SOME QUESTIONS TO ASK A POTENTIAL ADVISOR:

1. Are you independent?

2. Why did you recommend this fund or investment?

3. Are there any other funds, investments, or products which may better fit my unique situation?

4. Is this a proprietary fund, investment, or product?

5. How many companies are you contracted with? Do you receive any special incentives from any of them?

RECAP: YOUR FINANCIAL ADVISOR SHOULD ...

1. Be trustworthy, honest, and an upstanding citizen.

2. Be knowledgeable about your current situation, and be able to show you how they can better assist you. Professional certifications are helpful, but not necessary.

3. Uphold a fiduciary standard—which means they are fully transparent about their compensation and disclose any conflicts of interest. They are legally required to make recommendations which are in your best interest.

4. Be independent so they can work for YOU instead of a parent company.

5. You Want Someone Dually Licensed

I MAGINE A PILOT WHO KNEW how to take off, but didn't know how to land. Wouldn't that be strange? They learned how to read their instruments for takeoff, but when it came to landing, they had to ask another pilot to do it. That pilot would be out of a job real quick!

Along the same lines, there are some financial professionals who have one license that only covers one aspect of financial services and not the other. When it comes to financial advice, especially for retirement planning, there are usually two licenses which give the financial advisor the qualifications to put in place a holistic plan. Those two licenses are 1) a securities license and 2) an insurance license.

A securities license or registration, such as a series 65 or 66, qualifies the advisor to provide investment advice for a fee. Once an advisor passes one of these exams and registers, he or she is an Investment Adviser Representative. The insurance license gives the individual the ability to offer solutions which only come from the insurance world. You may be thinking to yourself, "I get the investment advice part. But what does insurance have to do with this?"

The fact is that there are some financial tools which only come from an insurance company. This would include certain types of life insurance and annuities which can be used for wealth accumulation, income planning, or certain tax strategies. Insurance companies manage a large portion of retirees' wealth. According to the U.S. Department of the Treasury, as of 2016, approximately $480 billion was invested with insurance companies just that year alone (https://www.treasury.gov/initiatives/fio/reports-and-notices/Documents/2016_Annual_Report.pdf). That's a big chunk of cash! Therefore, insurance companies have a big part to play when it comes to financial planning.

Aside from Social Security or a pension plan, an annuity is the only other financial tool available today which can guarantee lifetime income. An annuity is a contract between a client and the insurance company in which the company makes certain guarantees to the client. The most unique guarantee is that the client can receive a lifetime income benefit (otherwise known as a paycheck) that they can never outlive. There is no mutual fund or security of any kind that can make that guarantee. Of course, those guarantees must be backed by the financial stability and claims-paying ability of the issuing insurance company. But nevertheless, this puts insurance solutions in a class of their own—especially for those looking to do retirement income planning. It can be an integral part of an income distribution plan to use solutions which can guarantee income.

Did you know that there are some brokers who only have a securities license? And in the same way, there are some financial professionals who only have an insurance license. I believe that having both licenses is the only true way to be unbiased when it comes to making a product recommendation for you. Think of a contractor who you just hired to build your house. Imagine if you told the contractor, "I want you to build my home according to my blueprint. However, I want you to use every tool available except a hammer." Wouldn't that contractor be at a disadvantage? You're restricting him as to what tools he can use. The same is true for a financial advisor who is unable to offer certain financial tools. Each financial tool has a distinct purpose. The reality is that there are different financial vehicles for different purposes—and you need both an insurance license and a securities license in order to offer them all.

For instance, I've seen a gentleman who has become very famous for bashing insurance annuities. You will see his commercials on TV and he will tell you not to purchase an annuity. He will even offer to pay the difference of what it costs to surrender your annuity contract if you will invest with him. Why do you think this is? In my opinion, it's because he doesn't have an insurance license! Since he only has a securities license, he wants you to invest with him, and he can't offer you an annuity. It looks like he's bashing a product he doesn't offer just so you will decide to invest in his portfolio. In many cases, also, he will make more money over the long-term with his investment fees than what he would have made offering an annuity. Is this in the client's best interest? Everyone's situation is different, but you can see where I'm going with this. Don't be misled by commercials and fancy marketing—there's always an agenda.

The same goes for insurance-only producers. They emphasize annuities and life insurance too much, in my opinion. Why do you think that is? Because insurance products are the only solution they make money from! They can't offer investments of any kind because they are not licensed to do so.

You see the dilemma. Not only do you have to consider which company an advisor may be working for, or if they're independent, knowledgeable, and a fiduciary—you also have to look into the licenses they hold in order to determine whether or not they are the right advisor to help you work towards your financial goals. And if they lack one of these two licenses, then in my opinion they will be limited in how they can help you.

Most people, at least those approaching retirement, may need some solutions from both the investment and the insurance world. There is not one product or portfolio which will accomplish every goal, so you want to work with someone who has the wherewithal to help you construct a well-balanced strategy.

A short chapter, but an important one. Make sure you have a pilot who can not only take off, but can also land!

SOME QUESTIONS TO ASK A POTENTIAL ADVISOR:

1. Do you hold a securities license? Which one? (Series 7 and Series 6 are broker licenses. Series 65 or 66 are fiduciary licenses.)

2. Do you hold an insurance license?

3. What is your opinion on utilizing solutions from both the securities industry and the insurance industry?

RECAP: YOUR FINANCIAL ADVISOR SHOULD ...

1. Be trustworthy, honest, and an upstanding citizen.

2. Be knowledgeable about your current situation, and be able to show you how they can better assist you. Professional certifications are helpful, but not necessary.

3. Uphold a fiduciary standard—which means they are fully transparent about their compensation and disclose any conflicts of interest. They are legally required to make recommendations which are in your best interest.

4. Be independent so they can work for YOU instead of a parent company.

5. Have all the necessary licenses and registrations in order to implement a well-balanced strategy.

6. You Want a Team Approach

THE FLIGHT CREW IS AN integral part of every flight you take. The captain is by far the most important member of the crew, as your safety is in his or her hands. But on every commercial flight, there's also a number of other crew members who give the captain the ability to do the best job possible. In the same way, your financial pilot should have a team in place in order to give you the best customer service experience available. A team approach can be a huge advantage. When I was a broker, I was always surprised at how many advisors were one-man shows. They literally did everything themselves, and there's no wonder many of them got overwhelmed and some even lost clients because they weren't able to give the best level of service that every client deserves. So, what is an ideal flight crew for your financial flight?

We all know about the captain. His or her job is to lead the crew and successfully navigate the aircraft to the destination. Think of the captain as the strategist. He or she knows what it takes to implement an overall strategy to accomplish the flight's mission. In the same way, your financial advisor fully understands your personal situation, and will create a strategy to help you work towards your goals.

But with every captain, there is always a first officer. The first officer is also known as the co-pilot. The co-pilot assists the captain by offering his or her professional opinion on decisions the captain has to make. Not only that, the co-pilot might have certain responsibilities which lighten the load of the captain so the captain can focus on his or her job. Your financial advisor can be greatly assisted by having an additional advisor on staff who can brainstorm with them, perform additional analyses, or service existing clients on questions or concerns they might have. As it's always said, "two heads are better than one." No one is perfect, and a pilot and co-pilot duo can oftentimes do much more together than they can on their own.

What about the second officer? The second officer might be another professional who can assist the team in a unique way. Does your advisor work with a CPA or an attorney? If your firm has a CPA, an attorney, or both on staff, they have a great asset there for you. If a financial advisor has a CPA/attorney on staff, they understand their limitations. In this way they've made sure they are consulting with experts in the tax code and law. Financial advisors have a general understanding of taxes and the legal implications of your financial affairs, but they cannot give specific tax or legal advice. A firm who has a CPA/attorney on staff is a firm who understands the importance of a complete financial plan.

Another important crew member on a commercial airplane, at least in the past, before flights became more automated, was the flight engineer. The flight engineer was responsible for keeping the systems running properly. They made sure the engine was working, and stayed focused on fuel management. Think of the flight engineer as your investment manager. Any true wealth advisor understands the importance of making sure your investment platform is state-of-the-art. Unfortunately, the reality is that your captain and wealth strategist is in high demand. They are busy meeting with potential clients just like you. They are putting together strategies not only for you, but for a number of other individuals and families in the area. And let's not forget that they have relationships with their existing clients whom they have a legal obligation to as well.

The inevitable question becomes: if your advisor is busy talking to potential and existing clients all day, how can they be watching the markets and making sure your investments are performing properly? The answer is that they can't. That's what the flight engineer is for. They're making sure the plane is in top shape so that whatever the captain decides to do, the execution will happen flawlessly. The captain is the visionary—they know the coordinates and how to make sure the plane gets where it's going. In the same way, your advisor will help you choose your asset allocation, as well as create a big-picture strategy for you. But the flight engineer is the tactical expert who makes the overall vision a reality. A good advisor will go through a thorough vetting process in trying to find the very best money managers to handle your investments. They are the financial engineers (who often hold the CFA designations—Chartered Financial Analysts) who are watching the markets 24/7, analyzing the fundamental driving factors of the world economies, and giving the advisor everything they might need to help you determine whether any alterations to your investments are needed at any given time. If your broker is just picking stocks for you, do you think they're actively watching your portfolio all the time?

Don't be fooled. Consider hiring a team with the adequate resources at their disposal to assist you in making it to your destination.

So far we've covered that your pilot can be greatly assisted by certain co-pilots, as well as a flight engineer who handles the technical aspects of your flight's mission. But what about customer service? That's an extremely important facet of your flight experience, from the reservations desk to the flight attendants. The same is true for the financial company you choose to help you manage your life savings.

Have you ever called your advisor on the phone and got their voicemail? It's common that they are busy either speaking with another client, or working hard on designing a financial strategy. Therefore, if your firm has a client service manager, they will be a great asset to you. When you call the office, the customer service manager will be able to answer certain questions for you, or handle simple requests like distribution or other service-related needs you might have. If your firm has someone dedicated solely to client service requests, you will always have someone who can help get you what you need, even if your advisor is occupied. I cannot stress enough how valuable this team member is!

There can be a variety of additional roles on your pilot's team. Perhaps event managers, marketing directors, or other executive assistants. Each team member should always be focused on giving you the best client experience available. You deserve no less!

SOME QUESTIONS TO ASK A POTENTIAL ADVISOR:

1. Who is on your team? What are they responsible for?

2. Do you consult with a CPA or attorney when creating financial plans?

3. If you're on vacation, how will I get what I need if I call your office?

4. Is there anyone else who is licensed and can answer financial questions on your behalf when you're occupied?

RECAP: YOUR FINANCIAL ADVISOR SHOULD ...

1. Be trustworthy, honest, and an upstanding citizen.

2. Be knowledgeable about your current situation, and be able to show you how they can better assist you. Professional certifications are helpful, but not necessary.

3. Uphold a fiduciary standard—which means they are fully transparent about their compensation and disclose any conflicts of interest. They are legally required to make recommendations which are in your best interest.

4. Be independent so they can work for YOU instead of a parent company.

5. Have all the necessary licenses and registrations in order to implement a well-balanced strategy.

6. Have a team in place in order to give you the best executed financial plan and customer service experience.

7. You Want an Advanced Advisor

T HROUGHOUT THIS BOOK WE HAVE used the term "financial advisor" as a universal term for your financial pilot. In this chapter, I'd like to include another interchangeable term which can help elaborate on how the unique advisors truly stand out from the rest. The term advanced financial advisor refers to a smaller subset of financial advisors who specialize in several areas which go beyond the scope of just advising on investments. All financial advisors handle investments; it's what we're trained to do. But not all advisors may go into an advanced level of detail.

We've discussed how many financial advisors and brokers are merely product pushers. They are pressured to offer the products and solutions that their company finds most profitable, or those which are most profitable to them. When I analyze prospective client portfolios, I often see the same kinds of things over and over. It's not often that I can tell the individual or family at my desk that they are in good shape and there's nothing I can do to help them further (and if someone does say that to you, then you know they are honestly looking out for your best interest). The reason for this is because many people do not have a thorough financial plan; they might have a myriad of products or investments, but I am unable to see how it creates a cohesive plan. Your financial pilot should be giving comprehensive advice, not merely pushing products. There is not one product in the world which will solve all of your needs. You need a strategy!

All financial advisors and brokers are trained to handle investments. It's what they do! But an advanced financial advisor does more than just investments; they do complete wealth management. So, what does true wealth management look like? It includes investments, or what I like to call wealth accumulation strategies, but it goes a few steps further. I will cover them one at a time.

1) Income distribution strategies

Most of my clients are approaching retirement, or are already retired. One of my favorite parts of my job is helping to make life simpler for my clients. One thing that many retirees are concerned about is how they distribute their assets to live on. Do you just start withdrawing $5,000 a month from your portfolio and cross your fingers and hope you don't run out? (By the way, that's what some people do and have done for decades. This strategy, as of late, has been scrutinized by financial analysts surveying the current economic climate and most recent market cycles) Or, are there other income strategies which may help you better manage your tax implications, and further extend the longevity of your portfolio? One thing a good advisor should do is offer a detailed income distribution plan: show year by year and month by month which accounts you should consider drawing from and when, in order to give you the highest probability of making your retirement funds last. This can include various strategies which help promote the longevity of your money, all the while giving you a detailed plan designed to help you achieve it. When you see it written out, it can give you the assurance of knowing that you have a plan in place, rather than just hoping and wishing the best.

2) Tax minimization strategies

If your advisor isn't discussing tax strategies with you, then you may not be working with an advanced financial advisor. Has your advisor asked to speak with your CPA in order to put a cohesive plan in place? I've found that one of the biggest concerns facing retirees today is their worry that taxes may eat away at their nest egg. We all love and respect Uncle Sam, but we don't want him getting more than he deserves. If we can keep more of what we've earned, I'm sure we'd all like an advisor who could show us how.

3) Healthcare planning

Another one of the biggest concerns facing retirees today is how they will pay for healthcare expenses if they experienced a long-term care event. This is a loaded topic altogether, but there are a variety of alternative strategies that many people are unaware of that can help you fund long-term care expenses. While traditional long term care insurance may be right for some, I no longer offer it due to its expensive cost and the long track-record of insurance companies being forced to raise their premiums due to excessive claims. But there are a variety of alternative strategies which can serve a dual purpose and help retirees prepare for the wildcard of healthcare issues down the road. I have found that these solutions are not very common among financial advisors, as some just offer the most traditional solution—which may not be the right one for everyone.

4) Wealth transfer strategies

Of course, you come first when it comes to your money. First and foremost, you want it to be there for you should you need it. But for many affluent individuals and families, they're not going to end up spending every penny in their lifetime. A true advanced financial advisor will help you develop a plan with an estate planning attorney to help ensure that whatever amount of your wealth is left over, it goes to your family or a charity of your choosing. I'm sure the last thing you want is to look down from heaven and see a large chunk of your legacy end up in the pockets of attorneys and the IRS. A true advanced advisor will be able to strategize with you and help ensure you maximize your legacy and leave a lasting impression on the next generation, if that is something you care about.

SOME QUESTIONS TO ASK A POTENTIAL ADVISOR:

1. What is your philosophy on income planning? Do you offer detailed income distribution plans?

2. How might this strategy help me save on taxes?

3. What solutions do you have access to in addition to traditional long-term care insurance?

4. Do you work with attorneys to help them complete estate plans for your clients?

As you can see, there is more to a thorough financial plan than just a portfolio. Income planning, tax strategies, healthcare planning, and estate planning are all areas where your pilot has to be proficient and connected to other financial experts. I truly believe that a holistic financial advisor must be equipped with the tools, resources, and professional relationships in order to help you have a complete and thorough strategy that covers all aspects of your financial affairs. Once again, you deserve the best!

RECAP: YOUR FINANCIAL ADVISOR SHOULD ...

1. Be trustworthy, honest, and an upstanding citizen.

2. Be knowledgeable about your current situation, and be able to show you how they can better assist you. Professional certifications are helpful, but not necessary.

3. Uphold a fiduciary standard—which means they are fully transparent about their compensation and disclose any conflicts of interest. They are legally required to make recommendations which are in your best interest.

4. Be independent so they can work for YOU instead of a parent company.

5. Have all the necessary licenses and registrations in order to implement a well-balanced strategy.

6. Have a team in place in order to give you the best executed financial plan and customer service experience.

7. Be advanced in their planning—offering income plans, tax strategies, alternative healthcare strategies, as well as estate planning and wealth transfer strategies through their network of other professionals.

8. You Want Someone Who Can Do What You Can't

I F YOU HAD A PLANE and knew how to fly it, do you think you'd need a pilot? No, you wouldn't. You would have the ability to fly yourself to your destination. And there are many people who do that very thing financially: they are called Do-It-Yourself (DIY) investors. With the advancement of technology over the last several decades, it has made it much easier for people to become knowledgeable about how to manage their own investments. But, I think you understand up to this point that your financial advisor can offer much more than just investment advice. In fact, they *should* offer you a myriad of services such as tax, income, healthcare, and estate planning strategies as well. But nonetheless, there are many people who think that they can handle their own investments and do all of this planning on their own. And I'm sure there are some really smart people out there who do a pretty good job at it. However, I am fully convinced that many of them may greatly underestimate the value of an advanced financial advisor.

The reason why there are so many DIY investors is because it's possible to construct a decent portfolio in your living room. When I analyze some prospective client portfolios, I notice in some cases that if they just purchased an S&P 500 index fund, they could have had potentially the same, if not better, results than the portfolio their broker designed for them. This is why some investors have become DIY—because they realize that they may be able to get similar results without all the extra cost and aggravation. If having a portfolio which was directly correlated to the S&P 500 was all that's necessary for a financial plan, then yes, you could do it on your own. But I hope you have learned thus far that financial planning is much more involved than just a portfolio!

Understanding "sequence of return risk" is part of every retirement advisor's job. Sequence of return risk is the risk of drawing down too much from your portfolio at inopportune times due to the market's unpredictability.

For example, think of two brothers. One brother, Mike, retires in 1990. His younger brother, John, retires in the year 2000. They both have $500,000 in their portfolio, and they need to draw down $30,000 a year in income to supplement their Social Security. They both are DIY investors, and their portfolios both resemble the Dow Jones Industrial Average index. Mike, after retiring in 1990, has over $1.2 million in his portfolio by the year 2000. Not too shabby! Mike was a lucky duck. He more than doubled his money after his first ten years of retirement (even while drawing down an income stream). But John, after his first ten years of retirement, only has about $125,000 left to his name. Do you see the difference? Because of an unlucky sequence of returns, which were mostly outside of John's control, he has a real fear of potentially running out of money. A good financial advisor would be aware of this risk, and would position you in such a way that this risk can be minimized. At the time this book was written, we are currently in the second longest bull market in history. The market has more than tripled from March 9, 2009 to the beginning of 2017. Sequence of return risk is a real concern for those who may be retiring at a time when the next bear market could begin at any time. And while I am not trying to nor can I predict the markets, after every bull market, there is always the potential for a bear market, right?

I host retirement seminars at a few universities in my area. I truly believe there is a lack of unbiased retirement education out there, so I enjoy presenting these events to the public in my locality. From time to time, there will be one or two attendees at the event who love to ask questions and try to stump me. One individual just recently told me that handling his investments is "his hobby." Well, I have a few hobbies too. I'm pretty good at them. But I'm not a pro. It always scares me that people think they can fly their financial planes just because they've read a few books or watch CNBC on a regular basis. But if you can do it yourself, all the power to you, and good luck! I sincerely wish you the best. (Also, if you're of the DIY persuasion, some advisors are willing to work with you on a consultative basis, where you pay them an hourly or fixed fee if you'd prefer to manage your own investments. I highly recommend you pick a professional advisor's brain and not just try to "wing it.")

But I always tell my prospective clients, even the DIY investors, that I should be able to do something which they cannot do themselves, and I believe that with all my heart. If I just offered a basket of mutual funds—60% stocks and 40% bonds—then I understand that they wouldn't need me to help them with that. They can figure that out on their own. But the value a true financial advisor brings to the table is, in my opinion, worth their weight in gold. Here's why.

There are two divisions of many major financial firms: 1) a retail division, and 2) an institutional division. If you walk into a bank or brokerage house and ask to talk to someone about financial advice, you will meet that company's retail division. They will have a financial representative, a broker, who can offer you mutual funds or other financial products. But if you were a Fortune 500 company, and you went to that same bank or brokerage house, you would not sit in the branch and talk to a retail broker. You would meet at the firm's headquarters, and have a conversation with the firm's institutional division. The institutional division deals with the Big Kahuna's—the Fortune 500 companies, the pension funds, and the hedge funds. You wouldn't have enough money to sit at that conference room table as an individual. You're small potatoes to them. Some hedge funds have a minimum investment of $1 billion. As you can see, retail is all you can get because it's as far as your money can go.

Some of the larger fiduciary advisory firms and their advisors have access to institutional platforms. In other words, they are able to pool together their clients' resources and get access to the types of investment management that larger investors have access to—institutional pricing, execution, and money managers. It's kind of like going to buy a gallon of milk at your retail drugstore versus the wholesale club. If you buy your milk at the drugstore, you will pay more due to the drug store up-selling it for a profit. But if you get it at a wholesale club, you will get it at a wholesale price—as if you were buying in bulk, 50 gallons of milk at a time.

Wholesale clubs are an interesting phenomenon. They don't make as much money on their products, but they make a small profit on the membership fees. It's all about loyalty. It's the same thing with using institutional money managers or an institutional custodial platform. The cost can be greatly reduced for the quality of investment management that you're getting. Now, will that mean it will be the cheapest around? No! Do you want good, or do you want cheap? If you work with an advisor who has access to an institutional platform, then you will have access to money managers that you might otherwise be unable to access. If you find the right advisor, they can bring the institutional money management that big companies have access to right down to your kitchen table. Or, they might give you access to strategies that are unique and designed especially for people in your situation, like those approaching retirement and who are concerned about sequence of return risk. This level of institutional management may give your advisor the ability to give you a more custom, tailor-fit investment strategy rather than the run-of-the-mill portfolios, which are easy to imitate.

I always like to tell my clients that it's my job as your pilot to minimize turbulence as much as possible. My wife firmly grasps my hand during flight turbulence whenever we're flying somewhere. Some people do not mind it, but others get extremely worried when the wind is beating against the plane and the weather outside makes it difficult for the pilot to navigate. It should be no different with your financial pilot. You want to make sure that they are able to help you minimize market turbulence—the drastic ups and downs of stock market volatility. I will spare you the mathematical calculations, but it is verifiable that portfolios which minimize market turbulence often end up with more money at the end of the day.

You also want to make sure that your financial pilot can handle a worst-case scenario. I always ask my clients: Do you think we may have another 2008 over the course of your 30 years of retirement? Most say yes. I will always respond by saying that even if we were to have another 2008, I want to make sure that our flight plan can weather that storm. We can't just pretend and hope that it won't happen again. We need to be prepared in the best way possible. Am I saying that I can guarantee returns? No! But an advanced advisor should know how to position you in such a way that is custom-fit to your needs, expectations, and goals. And if your flight heads into a storm, your pilot should be adequately trained to handle a worst-case scenario so that you and your family survive and make it through.

SOME QUESTIONS TO ASK A POTENTIAL ADVISOR:

1. Are your investment solutions retail or institutional?

2. Are the investment solutions you offer exclusive or can I access them myself?

3. What sets you apart from most other portfolio managers?

4. What is your investment philosophy?

5. What can you do for me that I can't do on my own?

RECAP: YOUR FINANCIAL ADVISOR SHOULD ...

1. Be trustworthy, honest, and an upstanding citizen.

2. Be knowledgeable about your current situation, and be able to show you how they can better assist you. Professional certifications are helpful, but not necessary.

3. Uphold a fiduciary standard—which means they are fully transparent about their compensation and disclose any conflicts of interest. They are legally required to make recommendations which are in your best interest.

4. Be independent so they can work for YOU instead of a parent company.

5. Have all the necessary licenses and registrations in order to implement a well-balanced strategy.

6. Have a team in place in order to give you the best executed financial plan and customer service experience.

7. Be advanced in their planning—offering income plans, tax strategies, alternative healthcare strategies, as well as estate planning and wealth transfer strategies through their network of other professionals.

8. Work with an advanced advisor who can provide substantial value, and who has access to unique investment solutions tailor-fit to your needs.

9. You Want Someone Who Stays in Touch

W HEN YOU'RE ON YOUR WAY to your vacation destination, don't you like when the captain gets on the
speaker system and gives you an update? "We are currently
45 minutes from landing at your destination." Or, "Please
put on your seatbelt, we are anticipating some turbulence
up ahead." Good communication is essential to enjoying
your flight.

Oftentimes, I ask prospective clients what they liked or
disliked from previous financial advisor relationships. You
would be surprised at how many times people say, "I wish
when I called them, I got a call back." Or, "I wish they
called me and explained why my accounts were underper-
forming." Now, please don't think I'm perfect at this. In
the busy-ness of life, and running a business, it's virtually
impossible to call every single one of my clients on a regular
basis. I don't have enough hours in every day to do that.
But I do make it a point to put time in my calendar to call
my clients at least once every 3-4 months. And it's regularly
scheduled for my clients to have their annual or bi-annual
review meetings where we go over the progress we've made,
and reevaluate our goals and strategy.

It's essential that a financial advisor keeps their clients in
the loop. And sometimes, that isn't always by giving a phone
call. Our team sends out bi-weekly market commentaries to

keep our clients informed about what is happening in global markets. We send out a monthly e-newsletter and quarterly hardcopy newsletter to keep our clients updated on all of our events, as well as any timely articles we write. Our firm offers 8-10 educational seminars a year, all on different topics which affect our clients, whether financial or otherwise. We also try and do fun recreational events as often as we can in order to spend quality time with our clients and their families.

In addition, education should be of the utmost importance to your advisor. If you have an advisor who is passionate about education, then they are committed to not only being involved with managing your money, but also with bringing you up to speed on what's going on. You will always feel more comfortable if you understand the recommendations your advisor is making. None of us want to be completely clueless about what our advisor is doing with our money; being unaware of the advisor's reasoning is one thing that can end up hurting people.

Does your advisor only call when the market is going up, or do they call when the market is going down too? Not so long ago, the market had a global event which caused the Dow Jones Industrial Average to drop 900 points in two days. When it first started happening, we sent out a video email to all of our clients which explained what was happening. By the same time the next week, the market had recovered. Client after client wrote us and expressed their gratitude because they were really scared and weren't sure what to think. All they heard was the doom and gloom on the news, that the market was crashing, and they were worried. Your advisor should be proactive in reaching out to you in those times, not hiding in their office avoiding your phone calls.

SOME QUESTIONS TO ASK A POTENTIAL ADVISOR:

1. How often do you stay in touch with your clients?

2. How many points of contact do you make in a single year in order to keep your clients up to date?

3. Do you have any seminars or events scheduled for clients, whether informational or recreational?

RECAP: YOUR FINANCIAL ADVISOR SHOULD ...

1. Be trustworthy, honest, and an upstanding citizen.

2. Be knowledgeable about your current situation, and be able to show you how they can better assist you. Professional certifications are helpful, but not necessary.

3. Uphold a fiduciary standard—which means they are fully transparent about their compensation and disclose any conflicts of interest. They are legally required to make recommendations which are in your best interest.

4. Be independent so they can work for YOU instead of a parent company.

5. Have all the necessary licenses and registrations in order to implement a well-balanced strategy.

6. Have a team in place in order to give you the best executed financial plan and customer service experience.

7. Be advanced in their planning—offering income plans, tax strategies, alternative healthcare strategies, as well as estate planning and wealth transfer strategies through their network of other professionals.

8. Work with an advanced advisor who can provide substantial value, and who has access to unique investment solutions tailor-fit to your needs.

9. Be in regular communication with you, whether by phone, email, or educational events.

10. You Want Someone Who Takes Care of You

I MAGINE YOU WERE FLYING ACROSS the globe. It's a 20-hour flight. Would you rather sit in first class or coach? No brainer, right? First class is by far a more enjoyable experience. The seats are more comfortable, you have a dedicated airline attendant, the drinks and food are complimentary, and you have access to your own personalized entertainment onboard. We all love to be pampered, and there's a reason why people pay top dollar in order to have that kind of experience. The best flight crews take their first class passengers very seriously. They are always looking for ways to make the flight more enjoyable.

It should be no different with your financial pilot. As I always say, "Happy clients, Happy life!" I not only enjoy working with my clients in the aspects of my job that I find meaningful (such as helping people solve problems or pursue their financial goals), but I also just enjoy spending time with my clients and getting to know them. There's nothing quite like having that deep emotional connection with my clients when they tell me about their grandkids, or about their European river cruise vacation, or about their passions and dreams. You really can't be a financial advisor if you don't love people—you talk to them all day, every day! And in the same way, when you develop deep relationships with your clients, you really want to bless them in special ways.

Now, the reality is that financial advisors are actually restricted in how much love they can shower on their clients. What I mean is that there are actual limitations on how much money can be spent on each client per year. The regulators as well as the individual states in which advisors do business have strict limitations on how much money can be spent on client gifts, in order to avoid inducing clients to invest more money or to introduce their friends and family to their advisor.

Despite these regulations, good financial advisors find ways within the law to promote the most enjoyable client experiences for each of their clients. Does your advisor offer recreational events as gratitude for your business? They are great because a client community starts to build and friendships are developed with other people who are just like you within the client group. These types of events can make your relationship with your financial pilot that much more special.

In addition to events such as these, what about your experience when you enter your advisor's office? A friendly and warm greeting should always be the first thing you hear. Not only that, but I believe that a menu of refreshments and food should accompany your visit as well. You can learn a lot about a potential advisor by their waiting room's decor. Does it feel like you're at home, or is it more like a doctor's office? Client experience is more important than you think; a good advisor will make sure that your experience is second to none.

I remember when I first joined the firm I'm with currently. My mentor gave me a book on the Ritz Carlton hotel chain. She said, "Read this to get an understanding of how we treat our clientele." Have you ever stayed at the Ritz Carlton? The way the staff treats their clients is in a class of its own. You want to find a financial flight crew who will give you a Ritz Carlton experience. This so radically changed my life that I no longer say "you're welcome" or "no problem" to people. It's always, "It's my pleasure!" Everyone who works at the Ritz Carlton says it's their pleasure to give the very best client experience to all they are blessed to be able to serve. And your pilot should always find pleasure in making sure that you thoroughly enjoy your financial flight, whether in or out of their office.

But probably one of the most important connections you can make with your financial advisor is the confidence that someone will be there to help you manage your financial affairs. We have seen clients who, sad to say, were diagnosed with terminal illnesses or who suddenly passed away. The reality of this pain and suffering made us understand just how important our job is. They may cry in our meeting, not only because it is such an emotional time in losing their spouse, but also because they find comfort in knowing they have a relationship with an advisor who will watch over the financial affairs of those they leave behind. Like I said earlier, I believe that you want your financial advisor to be younger than you because one day you won't be here anymore. How special would it be if you could know that your advisor will be able to walk your spouse through the difficult road ahead, giving you the assurance that your family's financial affairs will be in order. And let's not forget the kids! They need help just as much if not more than the spouses we leave behind.

They may lack the experience of how to handle large sums of money, so if there's any legacy left for them, you want to make sure an advisor has their best interests at heart and can point them in the right direction to help them make the right decisions moving forward.

As you can see, there's a lot more to this than just dollars and cents. Choosing your financial pilot is one of the most important financial decisions you will ever make. On your retirement flight, all you want to do is to enjoy the ride knowing that you will have enough money to meet your lifestyle needs all the way to your final destination. If and how you get there can depend greatly on who you choose as your pilot.

RECAP: YOUR FINANCIAL ADVISOR SHOULD ...

1. Be trustworthy, honest, and an upstanding citizen.

2. Be knowledgeable about your current situation, and be able to show you how they can better assist you. Professional certifications are helpful, but not necessary.

3. Uphold a fiduciary standard—which means they are fully transparent about their compensation and disclose any conflicts of interest. They are legally required to make recommendations which are in your best interest.

4. Be independent so they can work for YOU instead of a parent company.

5. Have all the necessary licenses and registrations in order to implement a well-balanced strategy.

6. Have a team in place in order to give you the best executed financial plan and customer service experience.

7. Be advanced in their planning—offering income plans, tax strategies, alternative healthcare strategies, as well as estate planning and wealth transfer strategies through their network of other professionals.

8. Work with an advanced advisor who can provide substantial value, and who has access to unique investment solutions tailor-fit to your needs.

9. Be in regular communication with you, whether by phone, email, or educational events.

10. Give you a supreme client experience—whether in or out of the office.

There you have it!

T HESE ARE WHAT I BELIEVE should be some of the most necessary attributes of the *right* financial advisor for you. I wholeheartedly believe that each one of these categories is essential in putting you in the best place financially.

Now, will it be easy to find an advisor that fits all these requirements? Probably not. In my opinion, brokers are a dime a dozen. But a true wealth management professional, who is fully equipped with not only the resources but also the integrity and character which is required for your financial success—is out there somewhere. Now go out and find them! I wish you much wealth, success, and good fortune. May all your goals be achieved and enjoyed to the fullest!

—Richard J. Feola, CRPC®